# BRENDA KITCHEN'S

On the table *in* 20 *minutes*

**R&R PUBLICATIONS** MARKETING PTY LTD

**Major Credits**

Published by: R&R Publications Marketing Pty Ltd

ACN 062 090 555

12 Edward Street, Brunswick Victoria 3056 Australia

Australia wide toll free: 1 800 063 296

© Richard Carroll

On the Table in 20 Minutes

Author: Brenda Kitchen
Publisher: Richard Carroll
Project Manager: Anthony Carroll
Graphic Designer: Lucy Adams
Food Photography: Andrew Elton
Food preparation for Photography: Jenny Fanshaw
Food Stylist: Liz Nolan
Recipe Development: Brenda Kitchen
Editor/Proofreader: Sarah Russell

ISBN 1 74022 157 5

EAN 9 781740 221 436

This edition printed June 2002

Computer typset in Akzidenz Grotesk, Missive, Berkeley

Printed in Singapore

The publisher wishes to thank MasterFoods of Australia for the
supply of herbs and spices, sauces, salsas and mustards used
in the preparation of food for photography and for use in the
development of recipes and food testing in this book.

The publisher acknowledges the registered trademarks of
EFFEM Foods Pty Ltd used in this book, MasterFoods.

BRENDA KITCHEN'S

# On the table

## in 20minutes

# contents

introduction   4

magic healing foods   6

marvellous meat dishes   7

tasty chicken dishes   21

sensational seafood dishes   33

easy vegetable dishes   41

extra-ordinary eggs   47

delicious sweets   51

tantalising sauces   59

weights & measures   60

glossary   62

index   63

# Introduction
## Brenda Kitchen

The inspiration for my book comes from almost 20 years of creating recipes for 'Simply Cooking' and from my wonderful nan!

'Simply Cooking', my fresh food company that, for more than 15 years, has provided a service to major shopping centres throughout New South Wales. MasterFoods has been an integral part of the growth and development of my company. From the outset MASTERFOODS has supported my idea that home-cooked, simple food has widespread appeal.

After years of positive feedback from my fresh food promotions and hundreds of great recipes, the time was perfect for, 'On the Table in 20 Minutes'. My recipes, fresh produce and MASTERFOODS make for a marriage made in heaven.

In this book you will find simple recipes from my earliest memories to the present time. For as long as I can remember, food has meant more to me than merely a way to satisfy hunger.

Food has become my life and my passion. In *On the Table in 20 Minutes*, you will discover recipes that are fast and fabulous, plus slow, tasty winter warmers, such as Hearty Stew and Brenda's Irish Stew.

I hope you enjoy cooking my recipes and may the aromas of real food fill your kitchen and delight you as they do me!

*Food has always*

*Cooking with feeling ~ Brenda*

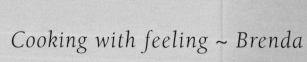

# A warm & wonderful world

My nan also played a part inspiring me to write this book. She created for me a warm and wonderful world in which food played a huge role.

*inspired my imagination.*

After our parents divorced, my brother Brian and I lived with Nan and Pa from when we were very young. We were raised in Clovelly, a seaside suburb of Sydney. The beach was a short stroll down the steep hill of Melrose Parade. I have fond memories of long summer days spent at the beach with my friends and returning home to good old-fashioned basic meals. I remember that Nan always cooked the best roast dinners for Sunday lunch. There is nothing like the smell and taste of a roast dinner after spending a morning at the beach!

*good old-fashioned roast lamb*

The Sunday roast consisted mostly of lamb with lots of crispy, baked potatoes, pumpkin, fresh beans and, of course, lots of gravy. It was home-made gravy, not the pretend stuff some like to call gravy. Gravy really completes a roast dinner and it's so easy to make with some simple ingredients and a little patience.

# Magic
## *healing foods*

**These foods have healing powers. Eat lots of them!**

| | |
|---|---|
| **Bananas** | Are an excellent source of potassium. |
| **Broccoli** | Is an excellent source of calcium and it assists calcium absorption. |
| **Cabbage** | Is known to contain cancer-fighting properties. |
| **Garlic** | Is nature's antibiotic. It is an energy booster for the immune system. |
| **Potatoes** | Are a fantastic source of fibre. |
| **Pumpkin** | Contains beta-carotene, an excellent antioxidant. |
| **Olive oil** | Moisturises the skin and is healthy to cook with. |
| **Onions** | Purify the blood. |
| **Spinach** | Is a rich source of iron and is high in vitamins and minerals. |
| **Tomatoes** | Are a rich source of antioxidants. |

**Fat** is needed in your diet. A little fat provides flavour and long-lasting satisfaction, which stops the need to snack in between meals.

*Have a creative time in the kitchen and relax by preparing early so you can really enjoy a tasty meal.*

BRENDA KITCHEN'S
## On the table
*in 20 minutes*

# marvellous
# meat dishes

# marvellous meat dishes

**Hint:** Usually Chilli Con Carne has red kidney beans but I've chosen to use the MASTERFOODS Three Bean Mix. It gives the dish a lovely flavour and different look and texture. It really tastes fantastic!

**Hint:** Irish Stew is delicious but you must use the best neck lamb chops. I'm not sure why their flavour is so very different from other lamb chops, however, I have found that if you don't use neck chops, you don't get the same flavour. If you want to make your stew extra creamy, add a little milk to the dish.

# chilli *con carne!*

### INGREDIENTS

1 onion, finely chopped
1 clove garlic, crushed
1 tablespoon olive oil
500g/1 lb extra lean mince
1 jar (500g/17¹/₂oz ) MASTERFOODS Salsa Dip – Medium
1 can (425g/15oz) MASTERFOODS Three Bean Mix, drained
1 MASTERFOODS Bay Leaf
1 green capsicum, finely chopped
1 portion (1 pack/8 portions) MASTERFOODS Beef Concentrated Liquid Stock
salt and pepper to taste

Serves **4**  Calories **511**
Preparation **10** mins
Cooking **40** mins  Fat **7.5**

### METHOD

**1** Gently fry the onion and garlic in the olive oil until softened.
**2** Add the mince and cook until it changes colour.
**3** Add the remaining ingredients and simmer for 40 minutes.

**Serve** with pasta, rice or vegetables. It can also be served with corn chips, grated cheese, sour cream and guacamole.

**Variation:** Create Nachos by lining a baking dish with corn chips, top with Chilli Con Carne and grated cheese. Bake in a medium oven for 20 minutes.

# brenda's *irish stew*

### INGREDIENTS

8 best neck lamb chops
3 large old potatoes, peeled and sliced in thick slices
2 large carrots, sliced
¹/₂ cup chopped fresh parsley
salt and pepper to taste
2 tablespoons plain flour
a little milk, optional

### METHOD

**1** Layer the chops, potatoes, carrots and parsley in a casserole dish. Season to taste and cover with boiling water. Put the lid on the casserole and cook on medium heat in the oven for 1¹/₂ hours.

**2** Thicken the stew by mixing the plain flour with a little sauce from the stew. Stir into the stew and place back into the oven for a further 10 minutes.

**3** For a creamy gravy, replace some of the liquid from the stew with a little milk after cooking.

Serves **4**  Calories **425**  Preparation **10** mins
Cooking **1¹/₂** hours  Fat **8.2**

pasta bake

# pasta *bake*

### INGREDIENTS

1 large onion, chopped

1 clove garlic, crushed

150g/5oz lean bacon, chopped

3 large mushrooms, chopped

1 teaspoon MASTERFOODS Ground Paprika

1 teaspoon MASTERFOODS Oregano Leaves

1 tablespoon olive oil

500g/1 lb lean beef mince

1 jar (300g/10oz) MASTERFOODS Salsa Dip – any variety

$1/2$ red capsicum, chopped

1 cup freshly chopped basil leaves

2 MASTERFOODS Bay Leaves

500g/1 lb spaghetti, cooked and drained

1 packet (500g/1 lb) grated tasty cheese

2 eggs

### Topping

1 cup grated cheese

2 eggs, beaten

1 cup fresh breadcrumbs, toasted

### METHOD

**1** Fry the onion, garlic, bacon, mushrooms, paprika and oregano in the olive oil until softened.

**2** Add the beef mince and cook over a high heat until it changes colour and breaks into small pieces.

**3** Add the salsa, capsicum, basil and bay leaves. Simmer for 30 minutes.

**4** Layer the spaghetti with the meat sauce and cheese into a large, shallow baking dish.

**5** To make the topping, combine the cheese with the eggs. Pour over the top of spaghetti bake, then sprinkle with the breadcrumbs.

**6** Bake in a moderate oven for 30 minutes until golden brown.

**Serve** cut into large squares with a crisp green salad.

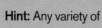

One of my favourite dishes Nan cooked was a huge spaghetti bake.

I was always starving! Food was a big deal and it was heaven to walk in the door and smell something delicious. Many of Nan's dishes come to mind but one of my favourites was a simple baked spaghetti. A delicious aroma would greet me when spaghetti bake was in the oven.

Nan always made a huge quantity! She used the biggest baking dish I had ever seen! Simple ingredients combine to make this old family favourite. The sauce was made from ripe tomatoes, bacon and onion. The dish was layers of cooked spaghetti, tomato and bacon sauce with a cheese, egg and breadcrumb topping.

One serving was never enough! Usually, I had two or more servings and only then did I feel completely satisfied! Although there were no microwave ovens then this dish could be easily reheated by putting the leftovers into a covered casserole dish in a slow oven.

**Hint:** Any variety of MASTERFOODS Salsa can be used to make Pasta Bake.

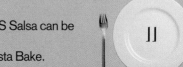

**Hint:** If you like spicy
pepper steak, then use
a generous amount of
MASTERFOODS Seasoned
Pepper or Pepper Steak
Seasoning. Don't forget to use a
tender cut of meat, such as rump
steak, T-bone or sirloin. Of
course, the secret to this recipe
is to press Pepper Steak
Seasoning or Seasoned Pepper
into your steak well and let it
sit for about 20 minutes.

**Hint:** Serve with
creamy mashed
potato and a green
vegetable. Wonderful
winter pie made with short
crust or ready-rolled pastry.

# creamy *pepper steak*

### INGREDIENTS

1 tablespoon butter

500g/1 lb rump steak,
trimmed

sprinkle MASTERFOODS
Seasoned Pepper

1 tablespoon fresh chopped
parsley and chives

3 tablespoons of fresh cream

salt and pepper to taste

**Serves** 2  **Calories** 108.5

**Preparation** 5 mins  **Cooking** 10 mins

**Fat** 3.4g

### METHOD

**1** Pre-heat an electric frying pan. Line it with baking paper.
When hot, put the butter into the electric frying pan.

**2** Add the rump steak and lightly sprinkle with seasoned pepper.
Cook until lightly browned, then turn and lightly sprinkle this side
with the seasoned pepper.

**3** Before the rump steak is cooked, add the parsley and chives.
Then, add the cream. If you want a lot of sauce, add all the cream.
If only a little sauce is required, add only 1 or 2 tablespoons of cream.

**4** Turn the rump steak several times in the sauce, season to
taste, then serve.

# hearty *stew*

### INGREDIENTS

1kg/2$^{1}$/$_{4}$ lb stewing steak, cubed

2 tablespoons plain flour

1 dessertspoon sugar

3 onions, sliced

1 teaspoon MASTERFOODS Freshly
Crushed Garlic

200g/7oz lean bacon, finely chopped

1 tablespoon olive oil

1 tablespoon Worcestershire Sauce

2 tablespoons malt vinegar

1 jar (300g/10oz) MASTERFOODS Salsa
Dip – Medium

MASTERFOODS Sea Salt Ground

MASTERFOODS Black Peppercorns
Ground

### METHOD

**1** Coat the stewing steak in flour and sugar and set aside.

**2** Fry the onions, garlic and bacon in the olive
oil until softened.

**3** Add the stewing steak and cook for a few minutes to
seal in the flavour.

**4** Add the rest of the ingredients, season to taste and
simmer for two hours.

**Serves** 6  **Calories** 328  **Preparation** 10 mins

**Cooking** 2 hours  **Fat** 4.7g

creamy pepper steak

*basic pie filling*   **Serves** 4  **Calories** 288  **Preparation** 30 mins  **Cooking** 30 mins  **Fat** 7.7g

# basic pie filling

## a meat pie story

### INGREDIENTS

500g/1 lb very lean beef mince

1 medium onion, finely chopped

salt and pepper to taste

1 teaspoon MASTERFOODS Mixed Herbs

1 cup water

Parisienne essence to colour

2 tablespoons plain flour, mixed to a paste with water

### METHOD

**1** Place the mince, half the onion, salt and pepper, mixed herbs, water and a few drops of Parisienne essence into a saucepan and bring to the boil.

**2** Reduce the heat to a simmer, cover the saucepan and cook for 30 minutes.

**3** Add the rest of the onion and thicken with the flour mixture. Add the flour mixture to the mince a little at a time until thickened. Adjust seasonings if necessary.

**Hint:** Parisienne essence is a colouring agent, available at your supermarket. Add more colouring, if needed, to give a rich brown gravy. Use this filling for meat pies with short crust pastry. Cook pies in the preheated oven at 220°C/440°F until golden — around 30 minutes.

Nan always decorated her pies with pastry leaves. She glazed the top of her pies with milk, mixed with an egg yolk.

During the 1950's in the seaside suburb of Coogee, Sydney, stood the famous Coogee Pie Shop. This unpretentious shop sold the most delicious pies with fine crisp pastry and a generous filling of rich gravy and mince.

Nan's pies are the closest to the famous Coogee Pie sold in the 1950's. Many gourmet pies are available today but the basic meat pie is still the most sought-after by Aussie pie eaters.

A home-made meat pie can be served with seasonal vegetables for a tasty and nutritious meal. Ready rolled short crust pastry makes pie-making simple. Individual non-stick pie dishes are available in good kitchen shops and some department stores.

On baking days, Nan would make cakes, biscuits and pies for the coming week's meals. The perfect leaves cut from the pastry to decorate the pies always fascinated me and I still make them for my pies today. They bring back warm memories of baking days during my childhood.

15

# moroccan lamb
## *salad wraps*

**Hint:** Using lamb chump chops' take all the lean meat off the bone. Discard the bone and visible fat. Sprinkle lamb with MASTERFOODS Moroccan Seasoning. To ensure the dish has the rich full flavour of the seasoning, don't overcook. This is a very simple dish, yet it tastes fantastic. It is a tasty, healthy and casual meal.

## METHOD

**1** Sprinkle the sliced lamb with Moroccan seasoning and fry in the olive oil for a few minutes but don't overcook.

**2** Combine the lamb and salad with the lemon juice and the extra olive oil.

**3** Put a generous amount of the lamb and salad mixture into the Lebanese or lavash bread and serve immediately.

## INGREDIENTS

**500g/1 lb lean lamb cut from 6–8 lamb chump chops**

**1 tablespoon olive oil**

**sprinkle MASTERFOODS Moroccan Seasoning**

**mixed salad leaves with extra rocket leaves and a few chopped mint leaves**

**3 tomatoes, sliced**

**Lebanese cucumber, thinly sliced**

**1 medium Spanish onion, sliced**

**1 red capsicum, thinly sliced**

**juice of 2 lemons**

**1 tablespoon olive oil, for dressing**

**Lebanese or lavash bread**

**Serves** 4  **Calories** 210

**Preparation** 10 mins

**Cooking** 10 mins  **Fat** 2.3g

# low fat
## *mini meat balls*

### INGREDIENTS

**750g/1²/₃lb lean mince**

**1 teaspoon MASTERFOODS Freshly Chopped Ginger**

**1 bunch fresh chives, chopped**

**½ bunch fresh coriander, chopped**

**1 egg**

**sprinkle MASTERFOODS Garlic Steak Seasoning**

**dry bread crumbs**

### METHOD

**1** Mix all the ingredients except the breadcrumbs in a bowl.

**2** Using a dessertspoon, form small balls. Coat the meatballs with the dry breadcrumbs.

**3** Dry-fry the meat balls in a pre-heated electric frying pan lined with baking paper. (Crumbed meatballs to be placed on top of the paper). Cook on high for 8–10 minutes, turning every couple of minutes.

**Serve** on a bed of iceberg lettuce with a bowl of MASTERFOODS Squeeze Tomato or Barbecue Sauce or any of the MASTERFOODS Squeeze Mustards.

**Hint:** This is a lovely recipe if you want to serve little cocktail meat balls before dinner. With a few basic ingredients, including the mince, fresh ginger and fresh coriander, you're giving your mini meat balls lots of flavour. Next time you're having a party, cook some mini meatballs and serve each on a toothpick. Serve with MASTERFOODS Sweet Thai Cracker Dip, fresh chopped coriander and a squeeze of lemon or lime juice, or MASTERFOODS Wholegrain Mustard.

**Serves** 6  **Calories** 353  **Preparation** 10 mins
**Cooking** 10 mins  **Fat** 9.1g

17

# supreme
## *bolognese*

## METHOD

**1** Heat an electric frying pan on high. Add the olive oil, onion, garlic and bacon and cook until softened. Add the mince and cook until it changes colour, breaking the mince up with a fork as you are cooking.

**2** Add all the remaining ingredients and simmer until cooked, cook for about 30 minutes or more.

**Serve** with freshly cooked spaghetti.

## INGREDIENTS

1 tablespoon olive oil

1 large brown onion, finely chopped

2 cloves garlic, crushed

1/2 cup chopped lean bacon

500g/1 lb extra lean beef mince

1 teaspoon MASTERFOODS Ground Paprika

pinch sugar

1 can (400g/14oz) whole Italian tomatoes

2 tablespoons tomato paste

200g/7oz mushrooms, chopped

1/2 cup fresh basil, chopped

generous sprinkle MASTERFOODS Chilli Flakes

1/2 cup red wine

1/2 teaspoon MASTERFOODS Sea Salt Ground

1/2 teaspoon MASTERFOODS Black Peppercorns Ground

**Serves** 6 **Calories** 98 **Preparation** 10 mins

**Cooking** 40 mins **Fat** 0.7g

*BRENDA KITCHEN'S*
On the table
*in 20 minutes*

# rich & tasty
## *pork chops*

### INGREDIENTS

4 large pork chops

1 dessertspoon olive oil

1 large onion, chopped

2 cloves garlic, crushed

1/2 cup chopped celery

1/2 red capsicum, chopped

3 small eggplant, sliced

1 jar (300g/10oz) MASTERFOODS
Chunky Salsa Dip – Medium

12 black olives

### METHOD

**1** Brown the pork chops in hot olive oil in an electric frying pan lined with the baking paper. (Chops are to be placed on top of the paper).

**2** Remove from the frying pan and cook all the vegetables until soft.

**3** Add the chops, salsa and olives. Simmer on a very low heat for 1 hour.

**Serve** with creamy mashed potato and pumpkin and a fresh green vegetable.

**Hint:** Lean pork cuts can be used in this recipe.

**Serves** 4  **Calories** 385
**Preparation** 10 mins  **Cooking** 1 hour
**Fat** 4.3g

# meat
*lovers pizza*

**Hint:** Press the mince onto the hot pan with another sheet of baking paper. This will make it easier to achieve the desired thickness for the base.

### INGREDIENTS

**250g/8oz very lean beef mince**

**sprinkle MASTERFOODS Seasoned Pepper**

**salt**

**2 tablespoons MASTERFOODS Tomato Salsa Dip – Medium**

**light shredded cheese**

**sprinkle MASTERFOODS Chopped Chives (or fresh chives)**

**fresh parsley, chopped**

**sprinkle MASTERFOODS Ground Paprika**

**Serves** 2 **Calories** 87 **Preparation** 5 mins
**Cooking** 10 mins **Fat** 2.8g

### METHOD

**1** Heat an electric frying pan on high until hot. Line with baking paper. Press the mince onto baking paper to form base of the pizza. Sprinkle with seasoned pepper and salt to taste. Cook, covered, on high until the mince changes colour. Turn the meat and continue to cook for a few minutes.

**2** Place the salsa, cheese, chopped chives, parsley and paprika onto the mince and cook on medium, covered, for 5–7 minutes or until the cheese melts.

**Serve** with vegetables as a main meal or with salad as a snack with crusty bread.

# *tasty*
# *chicken dishes*

# tasty chicken dishes

**Hint:** I've found that MASTERFOODS Salsa Dip makes a beautiful Parmigiana. Take a piece of crumbed chicken, cook it on one side until golden brown, then turn it over and put on a layer of the salsa (use about a tablespoon for each piece). Then top the schnitzel with some low-fat grated cheese. You could then sprinkle on some MASTERFOODS Chopped Chives and Ground Paprika for extra colour and flavour. Place the lid back on the frying pan, just wait until the cheese melts on top of the dish and you will find that the meat will be cooked right through.

**Note:** To vary this recipe, you can also use beef, veal or pork schnitzels instead of chicken.

## chicken *parmigiana*

### INGREDIENTS

1 dessertspoon olive oil

500g/1 lb crumbed chicken schnitzel

1 jar (300g/10oz) MASTERFOODS Salsa Dip – any variety

1 cup low-fat grated cheese

fresh parsley, chopped

fresh chives, chopped

sprinkle MASTERFOODS Ground Paprika

### METHOD

**1** Line the electric frying pan with baking paper and pour some olive oil, on top of the paper. Cook the schnitzel on high until lightly browned. Turn and spread some of the salsa on the schnitzel until covered. Sprinkle the cheese over the schnitzel.

**2** Sprinkle the schnitzels with paprika, parsley and chives. Cover the frying pan until the cheese has melted, then serve with potato wedges and green beans.

**Serves** 4  **Calories** 369  **Preparation** 5 mins
**Cooking** 10 mins  **Fat** 2.3g

## curried *chicken*

### INGREDIENTS

1 large onion, chopped

1 carrot, chopped

1/2 cup chopped celery

1 dessertspoon butter

MASTERFOODS Mild Curry Powder to taste

8 chicken drumsticks, skin removed

1–1 1/2 cups hot water

salt and pepper to taste

1/2– 3/4 cup low-fat milk

fresh chopped parsley

2 tablespoons plain flour, mixed to a smooth paste with a little low fat milk

### METHOD

**1** In an electric frying pan, lined with baking paper, soften the vegetables in the butter, add the curry powder to taste and cook for 30 seconds. Add the chicken, water, salt and pepper to taste and simmer on a low heat for 40 minutes or until the chicken is tender.

**2** Drain off some of the liquid and replace it with the low-fat milk. Bring back to a simmer, add the parsley and thicken with the flour mixture, adding it slowly and stirring until the sauce is the desired consistency.

**Serve** with boiled rice.

**Serves** 4  **Calories** 460  **Preparation** 10 mins
**Cooking** 40 mins  **Fat** 8.9g

chicken parmigiana

23

**Hint:** Why not make gourmet breadcrumbs by adding a few simple ingredients to store-bought breadcrumbs?

Experiment with the following:

1  MASTERFOODS Ground Paprika
2  MASTERFOODS Chopped Chives
3  Freshly grated Parmesan cheese
4  MASTERFOODS Mixed Herbs, Rosemary, Oregano or Parsley
5  MASTERFOODS Chilli Flakes and Garlic Salt
6  MASTERFOODS Lemon Pepper Seasoning or Lemon Grass and Chilli.

Make a super breadcrumb topping by mixing equal parts of grated tasty cheese with breadcrumbs, freshly chopped chives, MASTERFOODS Paprika and MASTERFOODS Chilli Flakes.

## easy crumbed chicken

# easy
## *crumbed chicken*

## baking *crumbed food*

### METHOD

**1** Slice the chicken breast into thin slices and place in a snap lock resealable bag. Sprinkle the chicken with lemon pepper seasoning. Seal the bag and shake gently until the lemon pepper seasoning is spread evenly over the chicken.

**2** Sprinkle in the flour to coat the chicken and shake in the resealable bag until it is evenly coated. Break the egg into the bag and hold the top of the bag securely as you massage the egg into the other ingredients. Now add the breadcrumbs and once again seal the bag and shake until the chicken is coated.

**3** Line an electric frying pan with baking paper and pour in the olive oil, on top of the paper. Add the crumbed chicken and cook until it browns. Add salt to taste, turn the chicken and squeeze on some lemon. Add the fresh chopped chives and parsley, then cover and cook for approximately 3 minutes.

### INGREDIENTS

**500g/1 lb chicken breast fillet, sliced**

**sprinkle MASTERFOODS Lemon Pepper Seasoning**

**1 dessertspoon plain flour**

**1 egg**

**dry breadcrumbs**

**2 tablespoons olive oil**

**salt to taste**

**fresh lemon**

**fresh chives, chopped**

**fresh parsley, chopped**

L ike most children, my boys loved crispy crumbed drumsticks — golden and crunchy on the outside, tender and moist on the inside.

I have never been a big fan of high-fat food and over the years I have developed some easy alternative cooking methods.

This baking method works well for most crumbed foods, such as chicken pieces, crumbed cutlets – veal or lamb, salmon rissoles and crumbed meatloaf.

Nan made her own breadcrumbs by putting any leftover bread on baking trays. These were placed in the oven to dry out in the stored heat often left over from cooking the evening meal. Nothing was wasted in Nan's kitchen — not even odd bits of bread!

*A great low-fat cooking method!*

**Serves** 4 **Calories** 316 **Preparation** 5 mins **Cooking** 10 mins **Fat** 2g

# easy chicken

## *stir fry*

### INGREDIENTS

**300g/10½oz chicken breast fillets**

**1 tablespoon MASTERFOODS Squeeze Sweet Chilli Sauce**

**1 tablespoon Hoisin Sauce**

**1 tablespoon MASTERFOODS Soy Sauce**

**½ teaspoon MASTERFOODS Chilli Flakes**

**1 red capsicum, diced**

**1 green capsicum, diced**

**6 shallots, diced**

**1 head broccoli, separated into florets**

### METHOD

**1** Slice the chicken breast fillets into thin slices. Line electric frying pan with baking paper and heat on high. Add sweet chilli sauce, hoisin sauce, soy sauce and chilli flakes and stir well.

**2** When the sauce begins to bubble, add the chicken fillets and stir to combine. Cook for 2 minutes, add the vegetables and stir-fry. Cover and cook for another 3 minutes, stirring regularly.

**Serve** with boiled rice.

**Serves** 2 **Calories** 68 **Preparation** 5 mins

**Cooking** 10 mins **Fat** 0.1g

# creamy
## *mustard chicken*

### INGREDIENTS

1 dessertspoon olive oil

1 dessertspoon butter

500g/1 lb lean
chicken breast fillets

sprinkle MASTERFOODS Lemon
Pepper Seasoning

2 tablespoons plain flour

1 dessertspoon MASTERFOODS
Wholegrain or German Mustard

2 tablespoons cream

fresh parsley, chopped

### METHOD

**1** Heat the butter and olive oil on medium heat in a frying pan. Add chicken, that has been coated in lemon pepper seasoning and plain flour. You can cook the chicken in strips or as whole breast fillets.

**2** Add wholegrain or German mustard, cream and parsley to create a delicious sauce and stir frequently. Extra light cream can be used in this recipe, if you want lots of sauce.

**Serve** with mashed potato and carrot and zucchini sticks. As an alternative to chicken, use veal, beef or pork strips.

**Hint:** Vary this recipe with the varieties of MASTERFOODS Mustards. I think the ideal one is the Wholegrain Mustard but you can also get Wholegrain Honey Mustard for that added sweetness. Or you might like to use the German Mustard, Dijon or perhaps even the Mild Australian Mustard or Mild American Mustard.

This dish doesn't have to be high in fat because you're only adding a little cream. I suggest using the light cream that is readily available in any supermarket and, of course, don't swamp the dish with cream, just add a couple of tablespoons.

**Serves** 4  **Calories** 192  **Preparation** 5 mins  **Cooking** 10 mins  **Fat** 3.3g

**Hint:** This versatile mixture can be used in several interesting ways:

1  As meatballs. Cook for 3 minutes on each side.

2  As rissoles. Cook for 5 minutes on each side.

3  As meat loaf. You will need to double the mixture. Cook in moderate oven for 1 hour.

**Serves** 4–6  **Calories** 201  **Preparation** 10 mins  **Cooking** 6 mins  **Fat** 0.9g

# thai chicken
## *meatballs*

## INGREDIENTS

**500g/1 lb chicken breast mince**

**2 tablespoons finely chopped fresh chives**

**2 tablespoons finely chopped fresh parsley**

**1 level dessertspoon MASTERFOODS Thai Seasoning**

**1 teaspoon finely chopped fresh ginger**

**1 egg**

**1/2 cup fresh white breadcrumbs**

**salt and pepper to taste**

**1 tablespoon cornflour**

**2 tablespoons peanut oil**

**1 teaspoon sesame oil**

**2 tablespoons finely chopped fresh coriander**

## METHOD

**1**  Combine all the ingredients except the cornflour and peanut and sesame oils. Form the mixture into mini meatballs.

**2**  Coat with the cornflour and fry in a small amount of peanut oil with a splash of sesame oil. Cook the meatballs for approximately 3 minutes on each side, until cooked through.

**Serve** with MASTERFOODS Squeeze Sweet Chilli Sauce, for dipping.

# crisp *chicken*

### INGREDIENTS

**500g/1 lb chicken plain flour
to lightly coat
chicken strips
1 egg, beaten
2 tablespoons olive oil**

### METHOD

**1** Coat the strips of chicken in the flour first and then the egg.

**2** Cook in the olive oil in an electric frying pan lined with baking paper until golden brown. This will take approximately 3–5 minutes.

**Serve** with a crisp green salad, roasted tomatoes and hot broken bread rolls.

**Hint:** You can vary this recipe by using fish or pork instead of chicken.

**Serves** 4 **Calories** 107 **Preparation** 5 mins **Cooking** 5 mins **Fat** 1.3g

29

# chicken
## *maryland*

### METHOD

**1** Coat the thinly sliced chicken breast fillets with lemon pepper seasoning, flour, egg and breadcrumbs.

**2** Cook on baking paper lining an electric frying pan in the olive oil until golden. Ingredients to be placed on top of the paper. Top with the ham, pineapple, cheese, ground paprika and chopped chives.

**3** Cover the frying pan and allow the topping to melt.

**Serve** with a crisp green salad and tomato wedges.

### INGREDIENTS

**500g/1 lb sliced chicken breast fillets**

**sprinkle MASTERFOODS Lemon Pepper Seasoning**

**plain flour**

**1–2 eggs**

**dry breadcrumbs**

**1 tablespoon olive oil**

**4 slices low-fat ham**

**pineapple slices**

**low-fat grated cheese**

**sprinkle MASTERFOODS Ground Paprika**

**sprinkle MASTERFOODS Chopped Chives**

**Serves** 4 **Calories** 297

**Preparation** 10 mins

**Cooking** 10 mins **Fat** 2.8g

# creamy
## chicken pasta

### INGREDIENTS

1 tablespoon butter

500g/1 lb chicken breast fillets, thinly sliced

1 clove garlic, crushed

generous sprinkle MASTERFOODS Chopped Chives

salt to taste

2 tablespoons fresh parsley, finely chopped

300mL/10¹/₂fl oz cream

sprinkle MASTERFOODS Seasoned Pepper

250g/¹/₂lb dried pasta

**Serves** 4–6 **Calories** 330 **Preparation** 10 mins **Cooking** 10 mins **Fat** 7.5g

### METHOD

**1** Heat half the butter on medium heat in an electric frying pan lined with baking paper. Add the chicken breast fillets, garlic, chopped chives and a little salt.

**2** Cover and cook for 4 minutes, stirring occasionally. Add the remaining butter, parsley, cream, seasoned pepper and finally the hot cooked pasta. Stir through to combine.

**Serve** in warmed bowls

**Hint:** This recipe is delicious with thinly sliced chicken breast fillets but if you don't have time buy a barbecued chicken with all the skin removed. Just use the meat from the barbecued chicken, combine with a little garlic and butter and proceed according to the recipe.

The other lovely flavours in this recipe are garlic and parsley. This is a simple but tasty dish that will appeal to all the family.

**Note:** FRESH garlic and parsley are a must for this dish and remember to cook your pasta to al dente.

# chicken
## *supreme*

### INGREDIENTS

½ chicken breast fillet per person

tasty cheese, sliced

bunch fresh asparagus or 1 can (340g/12oz) of asparagus spears

sprinkle MASTERFOODS Seasoned Pepper

a little plain flour

1 egg mixed with 1 tablespoon milk

breadcrumbs to coat

a little olive oil

**Serves** 4 **Calories** 312 **Preparation** 10 mins **Cooking** 10 mins **Fat** 5.4g

### METHOD

**1** Slice each chicken breast fillet in half to form a pocket. Fill with cheese, asparagus and a sprinkle of seasoned pepper. Close each breast with toothpicks and coat with the flour, egg mixture and breadcrumbs.

**2** In an electric frying pan lined with baking paper, add the olive oil and cook the chicken breasts, on top the paper, until golden brown. Turn and repeat. Approximately 4–5 minutes on each side, is enough.

**Serve** garnished with watercress and green beans.

# *sensational*
## *seafood dishes*

33

# brenda's famous
## *red salmon dip*

**METHOD**

**1** Mix all ingredients together well.

**Serve** with fresh chilled crudités, such as celery, carrots and cauliflower, all cut into bite- sized pieces.

**INGREDIENTS**

**1 can (210g) of red salmon**

**sprinkle MASTERFOODS Lemon Pepper Seasoning**

**sprinkle MASTERFOODS Ground Paprika**

**1 carton (250g/9oz) low-fat cream cheese**

**½ bunch chives, chopped**

**squeeze fresh lemon juice**

**Serves** 6 **Calories** 258 **Preparation** 10 mins **Fat** 2.85g

# italian
## *prawns*

### INGREDIENTS

1 tablespoon olive oil

1 teaspoon butter

1 small onion, finely chopped

4 cloves garlic, crushed

2 rashers very lean bacon,
finely chopped

sprinkle MASTERFOODS
Chilli Flakes

1 can chopped tomatoes

400g/14oz peeled green prawns

salt and pepper to taste

1 teaspoon MASTERFOODS
Ground Paprika

pinch sugar

fresh parsley

### METHOD

**1** Heat the olive oil and butter over a high heat
in an electric frying pan.

**2** Add the onion, garlic, bacon and chilli flakes.
Cook until softened, for about 5 minutes.

**3** Add the can of tomatoes, lower the heat and
simmer for 30 minutes uncovered, to reduce
the sauce.

**4** Add the prawns and cook only until they
change colour, turning heat up to medium.
Season to taste and add paprika and sugar.

**Serve** in small individual bowls with crusty
bread, garnished with parsley or stir through
hot cooked pasta as a main course.

**Serves** 2  **Calories** 91  **Preparation** 10 mins  **Cooking** 35 mins  **Fat** 0.95g

# whole
## *Thai fish*

### INGREDIENTS

1 whole fish per person

sprinkle **MASTERFOODS Lemon Pepper Seasoning**

1 tablespoon plain flour

2 tablespoons olive oil

300g/10oz **MASTERFOODS Sweet Thai Dip**

salt and pepper to taste

### METHOD

**1** Cut (or score) 3 openings on each side of the fish to allow the flavours to penetrate. Sprinkle with lemon pepper seasoning and coat with the plain flour.

**2** Heat the olive oil in an electric frying pan lined with baking paper. Add the fish (2 at a time) to the frying pan and cook on high for 5 minutes.

**3** Turn the fish and coat with sweet Thai dip, seasoning while cooking, then cook for a further 8 minutes or until the fish flakes easily.

**Serve** on a bed of jasmine rice, garnished with sliced cucumber, shallots and fresh chopped coriander.

**Serves** 4  **Calories** 615  **Preparation** 10 mins

**Cooking** 10 mins  **Fat** 1.6g

# seafood
## *soup*

### INGREDIENTS

2 medium onions, chopped

2 cloves garlic, chopped

1 dessertspoon butter

2 cans (400g/14oz) chopped tomatoes

1 cup fresh, raw seafood such as prawns, fish, oysters and mussels

sprinkle MASTERFOODS Chilli Powder

salt and pepper to taste

fresh parsley and chives, chopped

### METHOD

**1** Soften the onion and garlic in the melted butter in a large saucepan, add the chopped tomatoes and bring to the boil. Then simmer for 5 minutes. Add the seafood and simmer for a further 5 minutes.

**2** Add the seasonings, parsley and chives.

**Serve** in warmed bowl with crusty bread.

Serves 4  Calories 180  Preparation 10 mins  Cooking 10 mins  Fat 1.6g

**Hint:** This special sauce is great with this recipe. Here's how to make it:

### Special Sauce (Optional)
**Ingredients**

1 cup water

1 portion MASTERFOODS Liquid Concentrated Chicken Stock

1 dessertspoon cornflour mixed with a little water

1 teaspoon MASTERFOODS Soy Sauce

### Method

**1** Mix all the ingredients together and heat in a small saucepan until thickened, stirring constantly.

**Serves** 4  **Calories** 342  **Preparation** 5 mins
**Cooking** 10 mins  **Fat** 1.8g

# prawn
*omelette*

### INGREDIENTS
4 large eggs
250g/9oz peeled prawns
1 cup finely shredded cabbage
1 small onion, finely sliced
1 cup bean sprouts
1/2 cup finely chopped spring onions
2 tablespoons water
1 carrot, grated
1 teaspoon olive oil
salt and pepper

### METHOD
**1** Combine all the ingredients except the olive oil.

**2** Heat an electric frying pan on high, then line with baking paper. Drizzle in the olive oil.

**3** Pour in the omelette mixture on top of the paper and cook, covered, until set. Cut into four portions and turn each portion over. Season to taste. Cover and cook for a further 2 minutes.

**Serve** with Special Sauce (see Hint).

# easy
# vegetable dishes

# noodle
## *salad*

**Hint:** Prawn Omelette with Noodle Salad and jasmine rice is a fabulous meal!

### INGREDIENTS

**4 cups red, Savoy or Chinese cabbage**

**1 tablespoon MASTERFOODS Soy Sauce**

**1 red capsicum, sliced finely**

**2 tablespoons honey**

**1/2 cup chopped shallots**

**3 tablespoons Italian salad dressing**

**60mL Italian Dressing**

**1 packet (100g/3 1/2 oz) Chinese fried noodles**

**sprinkle MASTERFOODS Fresh Chopped Chilli, optional**

**1/2 cup slivered almonds, toasted**

### METHOD

**1** Combine all the ingredients and enjoy this fabulous salad!

**Serves** 4–6 **Calories** 259

**Preparation** 10 mins **Fat** 1.9g

# brenda's brilliant
## *rice salad*

### INGREDIENTS

1 large onion, chopped

1 cup frozen peas

1 cup frozen corn kernels

1 tablespoon butter

4 cups cooked jasmine rice

4 cloves crushed garlic

6 large prawns, cooked and peeled

2 tablespoons olive oil

juice of 1 lemon

3 eggs beaten with 2 tablespoons fresh chopped chives

sprinkle MASTERFOODS Mild Curry Powder

sprinkle MASTERFOODS Pepper Steak Seasoning

2 slices lean ham, chopped

fresh chives, chopped

**Serves** 4–6 **Calories** 280 **Preparation** 15 mins **Cooking** 5 mins **Fat** 3.3g

### METHOD

**1** Combine the onion, peas and corn and cook in the microwave for 3 minutes in a covered container with a dessertspoon of the butter. Stir into the cooked jasmine rice.

**2** Melt the remaining butter in an electric frying pan lined with baking paper and cook the crushed garlic until soft. Add the prawns to heat through, then add the prawns and garlic to the rice with the olive oil and lemon juice.

**3** Place the egg mixture into the frying pan and cook in a little butter. When cooked, cut into squares and add to the rice, with the mild curry powder and the pepper steak seasoning. Toss to combine, add ham and sprinkle with fresh chives.

43

## *the girls* & *the babies*

Ten girls and ten babies!—Our first meeting after the birth of our babies was at my place! We met during our pre-natal classes at the local health clinic.

This was my second child but for everyone else it was their first. During our last class, something said to me that supporting each other after the big event would be a great idea.

As the big day approached, my thoughts turned to food and to making our first gathering something really special. Being a show-off I wanted my dish to be spectacular! Well, I knew my mushroom pizza would be a big hit.

With its pizza base, home-made of course, topped with a tasty tomato salsa, onions, mushrooms and grated cheese and baked to golden perfection in a hot oven—my mushroom pizza was a real winner!

44                    *famous mushroom pizza*

# famous
## *mushroom pizza*

### INGREDIENTS
**Pizza Base:**

1 sachet dry yeast

1 cup warm water

1 teaspoon sugar

3 tablespoons olive oil

1 teaspoon salt

3 cups plain flour

**Pizza Topping:**

1 tablespoon olive oil

1 jar (300g/10oz) MASTERFOODS Salsa Dip

1 onion, sliced

mushrooms, sliced

a little more olive oil to drizzle over pizza

tasty cheese, grated

salt and pepper to taste

sprinkle MASTERFOODS Oregano Leaves

### METHOD

**1** Dissolve the yeast in the warm water with the sugar. Let stand until it foams. Add the yeast mixture, olive oil and salt to the flour that has been sifted. Mix to combine and set aside until doubled in size.

**2** Turn out onto a floured board and knead to form a soft dough.

**3** Press a piece of the dough about the size of a tennis ball onto a pizza tray. You could use a cone tray or even a large baking dish.

**4** Brush the pizza base with the olive oil, spread liberally with salsa, then add the onion and mushrooms. Drizzle with more olive oil and cover liberally with the cheese, salt and pepper to taste. Sprinkle with the oregano leaves.

**5** Place in a hot oven at 220°C/440°F for 20–25 minutes.

**Hints:** Use large field mushrooms, peeled and thinly sliced. Making your own pizza base is well worth the extra time and effort. Pizza dough can be frozen and used later.

Why not give this recipe a try:

### Gourmet Pizza Topping
**Ingredients**

fresh mushrooms, sliced

1 onion, thinly sliced

1 red capsicum, sliced

1 green capsicum, sliced

1 clove garlic, crushed

lean bacon, diced

a little olive oil

MASTERFOODS Salsa

tasty cheese, grated

### Method

**1** Combine the first 7 ingredients and mix well. You could marinate for a least $1/2$ hour before using on the pizza.

**2** Spread your pizza base with MASTERFOODS Salsa, top with a generous amount of Gourmet Pizza Topping and tasty cheese. Bake in the oven, pre-heated to 220°C/440°F, for 20–25 minutes.

**Serves** 4–6 **Calories** 496 **Preparation** 10 mins **Cooking** 20–25 mins **Fat** 6.8g

**Hint:** Use the All–Purpose Cheese Topping as a topping for Deli Hashbrowns or mix a little of the cheese topping through scrambled eggs. Alternatively stuff mushroom caps with the topping and cook in the microwave until the cheese melts.

It can also be used as a pizza topping, grilled on muffins, toast or as a filling for an omelette.

Place a little on top of cooked rissoles or chicken or veal schnitzel.

# all–purpose
*cheese topping*

### INGREDIENTS

**500g/1 lb low-fat tasty cheese, grated**

**sprinkle MASTERFOODS Ground Paprika**

**sprinkle fresh chives, chopped**

**sprinkle fresh parsley, chopped**

**sprinkle MASTERFOODS Seasoned Pepper**

**1 red capsicum, finely chopped**

#### Optional Ingredients

**bacon, onion and ham, all finely chopped**

### METHOD

**1** Mix all ingredients together and freeze in small snaplock lock resealable bag or refrigerate until ready to use.

**Serves** 8 **Calories** 204
**Preparation** 10 mins **Fat** 5.2g

# fresh *salsa*

### INGREDIENTS

**8 Roma tomatoes, finely chopped**

**1 medium Spanish or red onion, finely chopped**

**10 leaves fresh basil, chopped**

**sprinkle MASTERFOODS Garlic Bread Seasoning**

**salt to taste**

**1 tablespoon olive oil**

**30mL Balsamic Dressing**

### METHOD

**1** In a bowl combine all ingredients.

**2** Spread sliced crusty bread with butter and a sprinkle of garlic bread seasoning. Grill or bake until golden brown.

**Serve** the fresh salsa on the hot garlic bread. This salsa is good if prepared a few hours in advance.

**Serves** 8 **Calories** 98 **Preparation** 10 mins **Fat** 1g

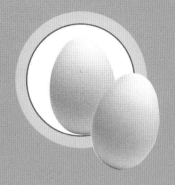

# extra-
## ordinary eggs

47

**Hint:** Finely chop ingredients such as capsicum, mushrooms, shallots or cabbage before incorporating into the omelette mixture. There is no need to pre-cook the vegetables if they are cut very finely.

**Hint:** Using a sharp knife, cut a small piece of ham from the centre of the hamsteak. Don't cut through the hamsteak rather, try to create a small area to hold in the egg.

# easy *perfect omelette*

### INGREDIENTS

4 large eggs

1 tablespoon thickened cream

3/4 cup All Purpose Cheese topping (page 46)

salt and pepper to taste

### METHOD

**1** Gently beat together all the ingredients in a small bowl.

**2** Turn an electric frying pan to high and line with baking paper. Pour egg mixture into frying pan, cover and cook on full power until set. This will take about 5 minutes. To turn the omelette, take two corners of the baking paper and pull to one side and your omelette will fold in half perfectly.

**Serve** with a little rocket.

**Serves** 2  **Calories** 268.5  **Preparation** 5 mins
**Cooking** 10 mins  **Fat** 13g

# easy *ham and eggs*

### INGREDIENTS

1 hamsteak

1 egg

grated cheese

sprinkle MASTERFOODS Ground Paprika

a little fresh parsley, chopped

a little fresh chives, chopped

### METHOD

**1** On a saucer place a sheet of baking paper. On top of this put the hamsteak and break the egg onto it. Try to manoeuvre the yolk to the middle of the hamsteak and have the egg white cover it until it partially flows over the edge.

**2** The rounded base of the saucer will help hold the shape of the egg. Pierce the yolk and sprinkle a little grated cheese onto the egg, then sprinkle with paprika, parsley and chives.

**3** Cover the saucer, put into a microwave and cook on high for 1 1/2 minutes or until the egg is the way you like it.

**Serves** 1  **Calories** 214  **Preparation** 5 mins  **Cooking** 2 mins  **Fat** 3.5g

*easy perfect omelette*

49

# toad
## *in the hole*

### INGREDIENTS

**4 slices bread, with a hole the size of a 50 cent piece cut out of the centre**

**4 eggs**

**a little soft butter**

**pepper and salt to taste**

**fresh chives, chopped**

**Serves** 4 **Calories** 148 **Preparation** 5 mins

**Cooking** 5 mins **Fat** 2.9g

### METHOD

**1** Heat an electric frying pan on high, then line with a sheet of baking paper. Butter the bread and place buttered side down in the lined frying pan. Cook until golden brown.

**2** Turn over and break an egg into the hole in each slice of bread. Season with pepper and salt to taste, cover and cook until the egg is set. Sprinkle with a little chopped fresh chives before serving. Turn again for a well done egg.

# delicious
## sweets

# fruity
## pan scones

## INGREDIENTS

**1 cup sultanas**

**3 cups self-raising
flour, sifted**

**1 cup milk**

**1 cup thickened cream**

**a little extra flour**

**Serves** 6  **Calories** 416  **Preparation** 5 mins
**Cooking** 17 mins  **Fat** 5.4g

## METHOD

**1** Add the sultanas to the flour, then add the milk and
cream. Using a knife, stir to make a sticky dough.

**2** Turn the mixture out onto a floured board, sprinkle
with a little extra flour and pat into a rectangular shape,
approximately 3cm/1$^1$/4 in high.

**3** Cut out scones with a scone cutter. Place scones
in an electric frying pan lined with Baking paper. Cook,
covered, on medium for 5 minutes.

**4** Turn scones and cook for a further 5–8 minutes.
The scones can be cooked in a conventional oven,
preheated to 220°C, for 15 minutes.

**Serve** with jam and cream.

# fabulous
## *fruit salad*

### INGREDIENTS

1 peach

1 green apple

1 red apple

1 mango

a few slices rockmelon

1 punnet strawberries

½ can/375g/13oz pineapple pieces with juice

generous sprinkle MASTERFOODS Mint Flakes

a little sugar to taste

### METHOD

**1** Dice all the fruit ingredients, except the pineapple and gently mix together in a bowl.

**2** Add the mint flakes and the pineapple pieces with juice. Gently stir through.

**3** Dust the fruit salad lightly with sugar. Refrigerate until cool.

**Serve** as a summer dessert.

Serves 4  Calories 78.6  Preparation 8 mins  Fat 0.1g

# granny's
## apple pancakes

### INGREDIENTS

4 Granny Smith apples, peeled and thinly sliced

2 tablespoons butter

2 tablespoons brown sugar

sprinkle MASTERFOODS Mixed Spice

$1/2$ cup sultanas

1 packet (375g shaker pack) pancake mix

icing sugar

### METHOD

**1** In an electric frying pan lined with baking paper sauté thinly sliced apples in butter and brown sugar until soft. Add a sprinkle of mixed spice and sultanas.

**2** Pour pancake mix over the fruit. Place the lid on the frying pan and cook on medium heat until firm. Sprinkle with icing sugar, cut into slices and serve with ice-cream, custard or cream.

**Serve** upside-down to display the beautiful glazed fruit.

**Serves** 6  **Calories** 279  **Preparation** 5 mins  **Cooking** 10 mins  **Fat** 2.8g

# rhubarb
## *& apple*

### INGREDIENTS

**1 bunch rhubarb, stems only, washed and chopped**

**2 peeled Granny Smith apples, sliced**

**1/2 cup sugar**

**3/4 cup water**

**sprinkle MASTERFOODS Ground Nutmeg**

### METHOD

**1** Place the rhubarb and apples into a large microwave-safe bowl. Add the sugar and water.

**2** Cook, uncovered, in a microwave on high for 15 minutes, stirring every 5 minutes.

**3** Sprinkle a little ground nutmeg over the fruit mixture.

**Serve** with cream, custard or icecream.

**Hint:** For extra flavour add fresh passionfruit after cooking.

Serves 4  Calories 155  Preparation 10 mins
Cooking 15 mins  Fat 0.1g

55

# banana

*surprise*

## INGREDIENTS

**2 tablespoons honey**

**2 tablespoons butter**

**sprinkle MASTERFOODS Ground Nutmeg**

**2 firm bananas, sliced into chunks**

**sprinkle MASTERFOOD Ground Cinnamon**

## METHOD

**1** Place the honey and butter into a microwave-container. Sprinkle the ground nutmeg over the top and in a microwave heat for 30 seconds on high.

**2** Gently stir the bananas through the warm honey mixture and cook on high for 30 seconds to warm. Sprinkle with a little ground cinnamon.

**Serve** with ice cream, cream or sour cream.

**Serves** 4  **Calories** 202  **Preparation** 5 mins

**Cooking** 1 min  **Fat** 3.8g

# curry
## *mayonnaise*

### INGREDIENTS

¹/₂ cup whole-egg mayonnaise

1 tablespoon finely chopped fresh parsley

¹/₂ teaspoon MASTERFOODS Curry Powder

squeeze of fresh lime juice

### METHOD

**1** Combine all of the ingredients and serve with any dish that calls for mayonnaise.

### Serve with

- Poached salmon.
- Steamed chicken breast.
- Cooked prawns on a bed of rocket and mesculin salad.
- Fresh oysters.
- Pasta with smoked salmon.
- Danish open sandwiches of chicken or salmon.

**Serves** 4 **Calories** 470 **Preparation** 5 mins **Fat** 5.8g

# basic
## *tomato sauce*

### INGREDIENTS

2 cloves garlic, crushed

2 tablespoons extra virgin olive oil

2 cans (400g/14oz) chopped Italian tomatoes

10 leaves fresh basil, chopped

sprinkle MASTERFOODS Ground Sea Salt

sprinkle MASTERFOODS Ground Black Peppercorns

**Serves** 4 **Calories** 354

**Preparation** 5 mins **Cooking** 10 mins

**Fat** 3.8g

### METHOD

**1** Gently fry the crushed garlic in the olive oil until it softens.

**2** Add the rest of the ingredients and simmer, uncovered, until reduced to half the quantity.

### Serve with

- Freshly cooked pasta.
- Vegetarian lasagne.
- Cooked crumbed meat, fish or chicken. Top with grated tasty cheese and grill until golden brown.

# sweet & sour
## *fresh vegetables*

### INGREDIENTS

2 cups mixed fresh vegetables, sliced (carrot, cucumber, celery, red capsicum and onion)

1 can (440g/15oz) pineapple pieces and juice

1 tablespoon MASTERFOODS Squeeze Tomato Sauce

1 tablespoon honey

1 tablespoon malt vinegar

1 tablespoon cornflour mixed to a paste with a little water

4 spring onions, finely chopped

### METHOD

**1** Blanch the vegetables in boiling water for three minutes or in a microwave in a covered container for 3 minutes with a little water.

**2** Combine the next 4 ingredients and bring to the boil. Add the cornflour paste and stir until thickened. Add vegetables and stir to combine.

**Serve** with fish, chicken or pork schnitzel or on a bed of jasmine rice. (garnished with the spring onions)

**Serves** 4 **Calories** 249 **Preparation** 5 mins **Cooking** 5 mins **Fat** 0g

# mushroom
## *sauce*

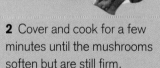

### INGREDIENTS

1 dessertspoon butter

1 clove garlic, crushed

250g chopped flat mushrooms

salt and pepper to taste

1 dessertspoon plain flour

sprinkle MASTERFOODS Chopped Chives

3 tablespoons skim milk

### METHOD

**1** Line an electric frying pan with baking paper and heat on high for a few minutes. Melt the butter and add the garlic, mushrooms, salt and pepper.

**2** Cover and cook for a few minutes until the mushrooms soften but are still firm.

**3** Sprinkle the flour over the mushrooms and blend with a fork, add the chives. Blend in the milk to create a smooth sauce. Reduce heat and simmer for 1–2 minutes.

**Serve** on hot toasted sourdough bread or crusty bread. May also be served over steak or chops.

**Serves** 4 **Calories** 165 **Preparation** 5 mins

**Cooking** 5 mins **Fat** 5g

# weights & measures

Cooking is not an exact science: one does not require finely calibrated scales, pipettes and scientific equipment to cook, yet the conversion to metric measures in some countries and its interpretations must have intimidated many a good cook.

Weights are given in the recipes only for ingredients such as meats, fish, poultry and some vegetables. Remember, however, that a few grams/ounces one way or the other will not affect the success of your dish.

Although recipes have been tested using the Australian Standard 250mL cup, 20mL tablespoon and 5mL teaspoon, they will work just as well with the US and Canadian 8fl oz cup, or the UK 300mL cup. We have used graduated cup measures in preference to tablespoon measures so that proportions are always the same. Where tablespoon measures have been given, these are not crucial measures, so using the smaller tablespoon of the US or UK will not affect the recipe's success. At least we all agree on the teaspoon size.

For breads, cakes and pastries, the only area which might cause concern is where eggs are used, as proportions will then vary. If working with a 250mL or 300mL cup, use large eggs (65g/$2^1/4$ oz), adding a little more liquid to the recipe for 300mL cup measures if it seems necessary. Use the medium-sized eggs (55g/2 oz) with 8fl oz cup measure. A graduated set of measuring cups and spoons is recommended, the cups in particular for measuring dry ingredients. Remember to level such ingredients to ensure their accuracy.

## English Measures

All measurements are similar to Australian with two exceptions: the English cup measures 300mL/10fl oz, whereas the Australian cup measures 250mL/$8^3/4$fl oz. The English tablespoon (the Australian dessertspoon) measures 14.8mL/$1/2$fl oz against the Australian tablespoon of 20mL/$2/3$fl oz.
The Imperial measurement is 20fl oz to the pint, 40fl oz a quart and 160fl oz one gallon.

## American Measures

The American reputed pint is 16fl oz, a quart is equal to 32fl oz, the American gallon, 128fl oz. The American tablespoon is equal to 14.8mL/$1/2$ fl oz, and the teaspoon is 5mL/$1/6$ fl oz. The cup measure is 250mL/$8^3/4$fl oz, the same as in Australia.

## Dry Measures

All the measures are level, so when you have filled a cup or spoon, level it off with the edge of a knife. The scale opposite is the 'cook's equivalent'; it is not an exact conversion of metric to imperial measurement. To calculate the exact metric equivalent yourself, multiply ounces by 28.349523 to obtain grams, or divide grams by 28.349523 to obtain ounces.

| Metric | Imperial |
|---|---|
| g = grams | oz = ounces |
| kg = kilograms | lb = pounds |
| | |
| 15g | $1/2$oz |
| 20g | $2/3$oz |
| 30g | 1oz |
| 55g | 2oz |
| 85g | 3oz |
| 115g | 4oz/$1/4$ lb |
| 145g | 5oz |
| 170g | 6oz |
| 200g | 7oz |
| 225g | 8oz/$1/2$ lb |
| 255g | 9oz |
| 285g | 10oz |
| 310g | 11oz |
| 340g | 12oz/$3/4$ lb |
| 370g | 13oz |
| 400g | 14oz |
| 425g | 15oz |
| 1kg | 1lb/ 35.2oz/2.2 lb |
| 1.5kg | 3.3 lb |

# weights & measures

## Oven Temperatures

The Celsius temperatures given here are not exact; they have been rounded off and are given as a guide only. Follow the manufacturer's temperature guide, relating it to oven description given in the recipe. Remember gas ovens are hottest at the top, electric ovens at the bottom and convection-fan forced ovens are usually even throughout. We included Regulo numbers for gas cookers, which may assist. To convert °C to °F multiply °C by 9, divide by 5, then add 32.

### Oven temperatures

|  | C° | F° | Regular |
|---|---|---|---|
| Very slow | 120 | 250 | 1 |
| Slow | 150 | 300 | 2 |
| Moderately slow | 160 | 325 | 3 |
| Moderate | 180 | 350 | 4 |
| Moderately hot | 190–200 | 370–400 | 5–6 |
| Hot | 210–220 | 410–440 | 6–7 |
| Very hot | 230 | 450 | 8 |
| Super hot | 250–290 | 475–500 | 9–10 |

### Cake Dish Sizes

| Metric | Imperial |
|---|---|
| 15cm | 6in |
| 18cm | 7in |
| 20cm | 8in |
| 23cm | 9in |

### Loaf dish Sizes

| Metric | Imperial |
|---|---|
| 23x12cm | 9x5in |
| 25x8cm | 10x3in |
| 28x18cm | 11x7in |

### Liquid Measures

| Metric millilitres | Imperial fluid ounce | Cup and Spoon |
|---|---|---|
| 5mL | 1/6 fl oz | 1 teaspoon |
| 14.8mL | 1/2 fl oz | 1 dessertspoon |
| 20mL | 2/3 fl oz | 1 tablespoon |
| 30mL | 1fl oz | (1 tablespoon plus 2 teaspoons) |

| 55mL | 2fl oz | |
|---|---|---|
| 62mL | 2 1/6 fl oz | 1/4 cup |
| 85mL | 3fl oz | 1/3 cup |
| 115mL | 4fl oz | |
| 125mL | 4 1/2 fl oz | 1/2 cup |
| 150mL | 5 1/4 fl oz | |
| 185mL | 6 1/2 fl oz | 3/4 cup |
| 225mL | 8fl oz | |
| 250mL | 8 3/4 fl oz | 1 cup |
| 285mL | 10fl oz | |
| 340mL | 12fl oz | |
| 375mL | 13fl oz | 1 1/2 cups |
| 400mL | 14fl oz | |
| 435mL | 15 1/3 fl oz | 1 3/4 cups |
| 455mL | 16fl oz | |
| 500mL | 17 1/2 fl oz | 2 cups |
| 567mL | 20fl oz | 1 pint |
| 625mL | 22fl oz | 2 1/2 cups |
| 1 litre | 35fl oz | 4 cups |

## Cup Measurements

One cup is equal to the following weights.

|  | Metric | Imperial |
|---|---|---|
| Almonds, flaked | 90g | 3oz |
| Almonds, slivered, ground | 115g | 4oz |
| Almonds, kernel | 145g | 5oz |
| Apples, dried, chopped | 115g | 4oz |
| Apricots, dried, chopped | 170g | 6oz |
| Breadcrumbs, packet | 115g | 4oz |
| Breadcrumbs, soft | 55g | 2oz |
| Cheese, grated | 115g | 4oz |
| Choc bits | 145g | 5oz |
| Coconut, desiccated | 85g | 3oz |
| Cornflakes | 30g | 1oz |
| Currants | 145g | 5oz |
| Flour | 115g | 4oz |
| Fruit, dried (mixed, sultanas etc) | 170g | 6oz |
| Ginger, crystallised, glace | 225g | 8oz |

| Honey, treacle, Golden syrup | 285g | 10oz |
|---|---|---|
| Mixed peel | 200g | 7oz |
| Nuts, chopped | 115g | 4oz |
| Prunes, chopped | 200g | 7oz |
| Rice, cooked | 145g | 5oz |
| Rice, uncooked | 200g | 7oz |
| Rolled oats | 85g | 3oz |
| Sesame seeds | 115g | 4oz |
| Shortening (butter, margarine) | 225g | 8oz |
| Sugar, brown | 145g | 5oz |
| Sugar, granulated or caster | 225g | 8oz |
| Sugar, sifted icing | 145g | 5oz |
| Wheatgerm | 55g | 2oz |

## Length

Some of us still have trouble converting imperial length to metric. In this scale, measures have been rounded off to the easiest to use and most acceptable figures. To obtain the exact metric equivalent in converting inches to centimetres, multiply inches by 2.54 whereby 1 inch equals 25.4 millimetres and 1 millimetre equals 0.03937 inches.

mm = millimetres   in = inches
cm = centimetres   ft = feet

| | |
|---|---|
| 5mm, 0.5cm | 1/4 in |
| 10mm, 1.0cm | 1/2 in |
| 20mm, 2.0cm | 3/4 in |
| 2 1/2 cm | 1in |
| 5cm | 2in |
| 7 1/2 cm | 3in |
| 10cm | 4in |
| 12 1/2 cm | 5in |
| 15cm | 6in |
| 18cm | 7in |
| 20cm | 8in |
| 23cm | 9in |
| 25cm | 10in |
| 28cm | 11in |
| 30cm | 12in (1ft) |

# glossary

**al dente:** an Italian cooking term for ingredients that are cooked until tender but still firm to the bite; usually applied to pasta.

**balsamic vinegar:** a mild, extremely fragrant, wine-based vinegar made in northern Italy. Traditionally, the vinegar is aged for at least 7 years in a series of casks made of various woods.

**baste:** to moisten food while it is cooking by spooning or brushing on liquid or fat.

**baine marie:** a saucepan standing in a large pan which is filled with boiling water to keep liquids at simmering point. A double boiler will do the same job.

**beat:** to stir thoroughly and vigourously.

**blanch:** to plunge into boiling water and then, in some cases, into cold water. Fruits and nuts are blanched to remove skin easily.

**blend:** to mix thoroughly.

**brown:** to cook in a small amount of fat until brown.

**buttered:** to spread with softened or melted butter.

**butterfly:** to slit a piece of food in half horizontally, cutting it almost through so that when opened it resembles butterfly wings. Chops, large prawns and thick fish fillets are often butterflied so that they cook more quickly.

**caramelise:** to melt sugar until it is a golden brown syrup.

**champignons:** small mushrooms, usually canned.

**coat:** to cover with a thin layer of flour, sugar, nuts, crumbs, poppy or sesame seeds, cinnamon sugar or a few of the ground spices.

**cream:** to make soft, smooth and creamy by rubbing with back of spoon or by beating with mixer. Usually applied to fat and sugar.

**croutons:** small toasted or fried cubes of bread.

**crudites:** raw vegetables, whether cut in slices or sticks to nibble plain or with a dipping sauce, or shredded and tossed as salad with a simple dressing.

**cube:** to cut into small pieces with six equal sides.

**curdle:** to cause milk or sauce to separate into solid and liquid. An example, overcooked egg mixtures.

**deglaze:** to dissolve congealed cooking juices or glaze on the bottom of a pan by adding a liquid, then scraping and stirring vigorously whilst bringing the liquid to the boil. Juices may be used to make gravy or to add to sauce.

**devilled:** a dish or sauce that is highly seasoned with a hot ingredient such as mustard, Worcestershire sauce or cayenne pepper.

**dice:** to cut into small cubes.

**dietary fibre:** a plant-cell material that is undigested or only partially digested in the human body but which promotes healthy digestion of other food matter.

**dissolve:** mix a dry ingredient with liquid until absorbed.

**drizzle:** to pour in a fine thread-like stream over a surface.

**dust:** to sprinkle or coat lightly with flour or icing sugar.

**entrée:** in Europe, the 'entry' or hors d'oeuvre; in North America entrée means the main course.

**fillet:** a special cut of beef, lamb, pork or veal; breast of poultry and game; fish cut off the bone lengthways.

**flake:** to break into small pieces with a fork.

**flame:** to ignite warmed alcohol over food.

**fold in:** a gentle, careful combining of a light or delicate mixture with a heavier mixture using a metal spoon.

**garnish:** to decorate food, usually with something edible.

**glaze:** a thin coating of beaten egg, syrup or aspic which is brushed over pastry, fruits or cooked meats

**gratin:** a dish cooked in the oven or under the grill so that it develops a brown crust. Breadcrumbs or cheese may be sprinkled on top first. Shallow gratin dishes ensure a maximum area of crust.

**grease:** to rub or brush lightly with oil or fat.

**joint:** to cut poultry, game or small animals into serving pieces by dividing at the joint.

**julienne:** to cut food into match-like strips.

**knead:** to work dough using heel of hand with a pressing motion, while stretching and folding the dough.

**line:** to cover the inside of a container with paper, to protect or aid in removing mixture.

**marinade:** a seasoned liquid, usually an oil and acid mixture, in which meats or other foods are soaked to soften and give more flavour.

**marinate:** to let food stand in a marinade to season and tenderize.

**melt:** to heat until liquified.

**mince:** to grind into very small pieces.

**mix:** to combine ingredients by stirring.

**olive oil:** various grades of oil extract from olives. Extra virgin olive oil has a full, fruity flavour and the lowest acidity. Virgin olive oil is slightly higher in acidity and lighter in flavour. Pure olive oil is a processed blend of olive oils and has the highest acidity and lightest taste.

**peel:** to strip away outside covering.

**poach:** to simmer gently in enough hot liquid to cover, using care to retain shape of food.

**purée:** a smooth paste, usually of vegetables or fruits, made by putting foods through a sieve, food mill or liquefying in a blender or food processor.

**reduce:** to cook over a very high heat, uncovered, until the liquid is reduced by evaporation.

**rubbing-in:** a method of incorporating fat into flour, by use of fingertips only. Also incorporates air into mixture.

**salsa:** a juice derived from the main ingredient being cooked or a sauce added to a dish to enhance its flavour. In Italy the term is often used for pasta sauces; in Mexico the name usually applies to uncooked sauces served as an accompaniment, especially to corn chips.

**sauté:** to cook or brown in small amount of hot fat.

**score:** to mark food with cuts, notches of lines to prevent curling or to make food more attractive.

**scald:** to bring just to boiling point, usually for milk. Also to rinse with boiling water.

**sear:** to brown surface quickly over high heat in hot dish.

**seasoned flour:** flour with salt and pepper added.

**sift:** to shake a dry, powdered substance through a sieve or sifter to remove any lumps and give lightness.

**simmer:** to cook food gently in liquid that bubbles steadily just below boiling point so that the food cooks in even heat without breaking up.

**skim:** to remove a surface layer (often of impurities and scum) from a liquid with a metal spoon or small ladle.

**slivered:** sliced in long, thin pieces, usually refers to nuts, especially almonds.

**stir-fry:** to cook thin slices of meat and vegetable over a high heat in a small amount of oil, stirring constantly to even cooking in a short time. Traditionally cooked in a wok, however a heavy based frying pan may be used.

**stock:** a liquid containing flavours, extracts and nutrients of bones, meat, fish or vegetables.

**thicken:** to make a thin, smooth paste by mixing together arrowroot, cornflour or flour with an equal amount of cold water; stir into hot liquid, cook, stirring until thickened.

**toss:** to gently mix ingredients with two forks or fork and spoon.

**total fat:** the individual daily intake of all three fats previously described in this glossary. Nutritionists recommend that fats provide no more than 35% of the energy in the diet.

**whip:** to beat rapidly, incorporate air and produce expansion.

**zest:** thin outer layer of citrus fruits containing the aromatic citrus oil. It is usually thinly pared with a vegetable peeler or grated with a zester or grater to separate it from the bitter white pith underneath.

# index

A meat pie story    15

A warm and wonderful world    4

All-purpose cheese topping    46, 48

**Baking crumbed food**    **24**

Banana pancakes    57

Banana surprise    56

Basic pie filling    14, 15

Basic tomato sauce    59

Black forest magic    58

Brenda's brilliant rice salad    43

Brenda's famous red salmon dip    34

Brenda's irish stew    8

Thai chicken meatballs    28

Chicken maryland    30

Chicken parmigiana    22, 23

Chicken supreme    32

Chilli con carne!    8, 9

Creamy chicken pasta    31

Creamy mustard chicken    27

Creamy pepper steak    12, 13

Crisp chicken    29

Curried chicken    22

Curry mayonnaise    59

**Delicious sweets**    **51–58**

Easy chicken stir fry    26

Easy crumbed chicken    24, 25

Easy ham and eggs    48

Easy perfect omelette    48, 49

**Easy vegetable dishes**    **41–46**

**Extra-ordinary eggs**    **47–50**

Fabulous fruit salad    53

Famous mushroom pizza    44, 45

Fresh salsa    46

Fruity pan scones    52

**Glossary**    **61**

Good old-fashioned roast lamb    5

Granny's apple pancakes    54

Hearty stew    12

Introduction    4

Italian prawns    35

Low-fat mini meat balls    17

Magic healing foods    6

**Marvellous meat dishes**    **7–20**

Master soy fish    37

Meat lovers pizza    20

Moroccan lamb salad wraps    16

Mushroom sauce    59

**Nan's spaghetti bake**    **11**

Noodle salad    42

Pasta bake    10, 11

Prawn omelette    40, 42

Rhurbarb & apple    55

Rich & tasty pork chops    19

Saucy smoked fish    38

Seafood soup    39

**Sensational seafood dishes**    **33–40**

Supreme bolognese    18

Sweet & sour fresh vegetables    59

**Tasty chicken dishes**    **21–32**

**Tantalising sauces**    **60**

**The girls & the babies**    **44**

Thai chicken meatballs    28

Toad in the hole    50

**Weights and measures**    **60–61**

Whole Thai fish    36

# Products *available*

With hundreds of products like mustards, marinades, sauces and spices, any cook can turn a simple meal into something special with MASTERFOODS. The entire range is full of flavour and easy to use, so even the busiest person can enjoy getting creative in the kitchen. They've been around for years, so you know you can rely on the quality. Try something quick and tasty from the MASTERFOODS range whenever you cook, then sit back and watch the compliments roll in.

With MASTERFOODS Sauces, Mustards, Herbs and Spices, bringing authentic flavour to everything you cook is easy. Keep a range of the MASTERFOODS products in your fridge or pantry and you can bring life to even the simplest food in minutes—even the humble toasted sandwich.

## Condiments

The MASTERFOODS range of condiments helps busy cooks give their meals extra flavour. Lift a simple steak with any of our mustards, from classic French and Australian styles to gourmet seeded or herb and tomato varieties. A MASTERFOODS Pickle goes well with sandwiches or you could even try a dollop of chutney. Virtually any meat is enhanced with MASTERFOODS Relishes.

MASTERFOODS products can also lift a toasty occasion. Give a garlicky toasted focaccia an extra dimension with MASTERFOODS Tomato and Chilli Pickle or try a squeeze of American Mustard and some freshly ground black pepper on the ever-popular steak sandwich. You can even create Indian-style wraps with some naan bread, chicken and MASTERFOODS Mango Chutney. With hundreds of MASTERFOODS products to choose from, there's no stopping you getting creative in the kitchen!